81

Mygrations

W.K. Buckley

FITHIAN PRESS · SANTA BARBARA · 1998

The following poems in *81 Mygrations* have appeared elsewhere:
  "Cannibal Review"—*Atom Mind*
  "C-street to cannery" and "Daydreamer on the line"—*Main Street Rag*
  "Edge Sideways Athena"—*Neovictorian/Cochlea*
  "faces West"—last section in *The Cafe Review*
  "Gestapo Sandwich"—*Coe Review*
  "Hanging Coffins"—*New Orleans Review*
  "In yellow rooms"—*Lynx Eye*
  "Lake Michigan"—*California Quarterly*
  "Lover in a Milltown"—*Main Street Rag*
  "Love unemployed"—*Atom Mind*
  "Off San Clemente"—*Night Roses*
  "Orange Quarters"—*Graffiti Rag*
  "Steeltown Love"—*Lynx Eye*
  "Skin Diving"—*The Cafe Review*
  "Struck once"—*Liberal and Fine Arts Review*
  "Southern detour"—*Main Street Rag*
  "Vertical"—*Melting Trees Review*

"*Baud*-sonnets" are numbers 6 and 7 from *Meditations on the Grid* (Alpha Beat Press, 1995)
"Love unemployed" printed in *By the Horses Before The Rains* (Small Poetry Press, 1996): winner of *Modern Poetry*'s "Best Chapbook for 1997."

Published by Fithian Press
A division of Daniel and Daniel, Publishers, Inc.
Post Office Box 1525
Santa Barbara, CA 93102

Printed in Canada

Book design: Eric Larson

LIBRARY OF CONGRESS CATALOGING-IN-PUBLICATION DATA
Buckley, William K., 1946–
  81 mygrations / W.K. Buckley
    p.   cm.
  ISBN 1-56474-241-5 (alk. paper)
  1. Automobile travel—United States—Poetry. 2. Landscape—United States—Poetry.   I. Title.
PS3552.U3445A614   1998
811'.54—dc21   97-39854
                                          CIP

Contents

Shut your eyes, that's all that is necessary.
        There you have life seen from the other side.
                            Céline

...at the foot of the Rockies, looking west over the desert,
        one just knows that all Pale-face and Hebraic monotheistic
        insistence is a dead letter.
                            D.H. Lawrence

—a woman's voice, a man's voice or
        voice of the freeway, night after night...
                            Adrienne Rich

SOUTH

South

Near from where migrants begin,
up from the sands of Imperial Valley & sunsets
the color of sliced melon, over Vallecito Mountains
& down to Cabrillo's Pacific,   coming
to the shores of Coronado a NEW SELF
spotted 34° 20'
                    —a brain cloud in its skiff—

navigating over silver-tipped foam,
pulling legs up from the kelp for the here in its orange.
Knocked fresh in his boat by grey whale, and sloshing in the
tidal pools seeing in the anemone & limpets
the tug of salinity,   this self darts in the oleander like
Digueño Indians, up to Presidio Park, & spies
east-bound roads to the mountains.
                    CALIFIA
where I took signals from the spouts off Point Loma.

Fogland

See if you can the current of street—
to leave headlands where waters boil in the Baja calvings,
this *hidalgo-lad* bred at a moment's notice to serve City:
his inner astrolabe in the infant Splash Zone,
the habitat where sea-whispers echo in the ear,
where he grows tanned & ideal in the Zone of High Tides
with sea snails and clawed crabs: until he finds
in the lowest tides the abandoned ocher seastar,
with its arms   *pointing East*   pointing South.

                    These first things
of imago migrate in the blood to adult—
the red algae of *Idea*. Packed separate from Father
& nourished by Mother. Bewildering to sisters like sponge.
The mean sea-level of his feelings that beachcomb his heart.

Caravel

Out from the school doors I would run to the piers
& imagine a fleet of full-masted barkentines
in the colors of Spain: the battle of *La Noche Triste*.

The slaughter of Lake Texcoco the slaughter of days
in unimaginative rooms—where the New World
      is Old. And the books I carry
on streets I was told were the keys to my freedom.
Smell of pages & glue the institutional opium
dispensed by the Keepers of roads & bosses of Cities.
My 10 yr. old nightmare of *Conquistadores* clanking in dreams
had jasmine coming in on the wind through my room,

& my caravel—pushed out from a skyline of glass,
anchors in kelp   to the roar of jet plane & the wave.

Girl

Then I out a window as she arrived:
the one who makes you forget your first dreams.
A Cajun from New Orleans whose mother drove West for gold
& I shoved Donatello's head to the wall
for a lick from her tongue. And those dark amber eyes
a sweet drip down my spine.   In November
she raps on my window . . . *her cherry lips glowing in a sea-mist*
& asks me to climb out.   I step down
                on Father's rose garden
& we walk Nautilus St. to the tides, her silver-tipped
shoulders gone glossy under sea-moon, & on reefs the lash
        of foam to her question for kiss—

I knew in my refusal it was she who with sea
      put the rhymed line in my bone.

Canvassing

Streets are like fault lines when you're selling
downtown in July. The overcast smell
of our harbors. Father bought me a briefcase
with brass buckles, stuffed with his *goods*:
Xerox paper, & parts, good looks & a future.
I canvassed C-Street after school in the fog
        & the Voices pounding under my feet
like the bilge pumps on an old cruise ship for fat cats.

On Broadway I'd stop cold for a beer & a taco,
the smell of erotica in X-rated movie houses,
the sound of bums coughing in Balboa Park
or the squeal of whores with their Navy delights.
        I'd lean up against buildings,
take a bus in the rain, watch the rich in their Cadillac limos.

Old Town

Down from Mission Hills to the valley of *Old Town*,
to adobe dwellings & cafes with saddles on walls,
the middle-class white boys come for the noise.
They flee from the ticking clocks in their rooms
to clash with their brown Mexican girls—
        where the roads look like EXITS
& the eucalyptus is slip-smooth with adventure.
Where the old bones of Indians still sleep in their massacre,
& the Spaniard God still speaks in the museums.

At noon, under the lemon trees, the Mexican-dances
in white dresses & the stab of *bougainvillea*.
And at night, in trumpets, the moon on tiled roofs,
the careless brown arm around waists . . .
        I'm dizzy
with jasmine in my *loco* on the San Andreas.

C-street to cannery

I canvassed streets in selling off dreams
like some corner boy with an angle/
cat-hauled Customers with a slit in the seam
of my pants & sweat in my hair/ until bus
No. 3 took me home/ where Crystal Pier rots in its timbers
& the railing all rusted as the necklace of a
        DEAD BOG QUEEN
My figures wouldn't add up—& to
my sense-around Utopia/& monotony of Paradise/
where coyotes stalk rabbits in their backyard pet-cages
came those bells & those whistles/& smell of fish
        at $6.50/hr.

With a top-down Chevy & its black leather seats
real toil in this cannery is the dickering maintenance
of my imagery/   like some limber Sisyphus, a

Day dreamer on the line/

The "gold shift" they call it, because the sun
would turn the sheds yellow at dusk/
& I'd drive with my windows rolled good &
down for the mist/before standing on lines/
where cans shoved to their holding bins
would wait for the Labeler—like Leda for Zeus—

& I would hear those unbearable gifts from Olympus/
those unbearable claims in the noise/
       & now I'm certain about *naming*
100% pure   Servings about 2   Canned in delight

In the longing-arts sand is the *color* of our hands/
blue-water the *birth* of our world/this our *shackle* of earth/
      minor keys of killdeers/this *jacket* of night/
        the *unchecked necessity* of Jupiter's rings

Calexico

It came to me early the big rolling wheel
of my business is the god-bus. of U.S./
& the grab-bag father worked for with its slithering coins
in the flames of his nightmare his school for my bones:
      —I graduated commodity-son—
magnum cum laude in prices controlled/& the same coin tossed
into the motherless cup is fingered by the bankers of Manhattan/

I'm thin enough to make change & go looking on roads
for a campaign of shadow/under bldgs. in their material shells/
      until I kissed stones & saguaros
& wondered if they could hold language/take contracts & give
      bids/

      & then Rosie in Calexico
woke me with brown hands for those white lights
strung up on the adobe/& the sidewalk sticky with fruit/

Dream-father

Father is buried on Point Cabrillo. His grave looks
down on a harbor where Imperial battleships rust:
and their dead soldiers wander the streets of San Diego—
their armor clanking through malls,
their mouths watering for gold in the Wal-Mart jewelry stores,
their boots knocking down doors for a drink!

Dream-Father, migrant-Irish face from New York,
you slapped me on the back & said: *"Go grease the Customer.*
Be brief. Put on your suit & I'll show you the ropes"—
I learned his lonely old tricks. I put on my armor

but stopped for a drink.   And when I
welded pipe, put down brick, or worked with cement,
it was then that I wouldn't   *grease.*

Dream-mother

I found comfort in declaring
that I had fallen from a mysterious womb,
in the year with radiation still floating.

(When Mother picked up her *Atomic Lebensborn*
& brought him to bedrooms papered with blue roses,
he felt *social*   **inconspicuous**   with her
sheltering graces, picking lint from his lapels before
"dates" with those daughters of Amoco.

And even when Dream-sisters in white dresses
after being kissed by the boys hid in rooms
tell him what they thought of genitals or running away,
it was always her restlessness—stoking his brain.
As if somehow she could
              make voyages   before death   in his exit).

Clear Sights

These years of *chula vistas* on roads going East.
From the stink of canneries & coconut oil on skin,
from the deadbeat deliveries of suburbs & offices,
from the bang of school bells & doors slammed in anger,
from roads driven visionary to the lip of cliffs,
from those plain rich-girls & their mothers & fathers,

I—drugged-happy & spine-braced—stood in the Ocean
& looked up to Mt. Soledad from The Shores—
heard test-engines of missiles rumble lovely
& muffled.   *My courtship is finished.*

Like surf grass, I feel migrant.
I dream of the *Pequod* with A-Bombs in her cargo.
And the appeal of the Exit . . . a nice trick.

Off San Clemente

To be cold, wet, & seventeen.
To realize dreams washed up on shores
where the backwash is treacherous.

Where Cabrillo first put down his boot
& felt it sink to the land Cortez stabbed.
And the flag he planted did not fool the condor,
who flew high like U2s & stretched wing for the soldiers.

For God & gold they broke through the jasmine,
& when they thought they had found El Dorado
the heads severed for a Phallic Queen
were kicked rolling to the surf.

You grow up by the sea. You believe in dreams.
You believe in promise.
Those paradisiacal waves should have given
death garlands, & love made by tanned limbs
should have undermined their voyage.

The Years

Down these tossed events
those migratory moments of the self,
when the choice you expect to make
is the instinctual-wave,   taken
by moonlight [deaf] to the Guardians.

The swim deep I think=my sanguined-splay
& this City fixed in hollows is gaged by brail.

Out of the clinics, out of the schools I'm mustered
by the inner toll, a central expectation denied,
the silent *public distich* [here] delayed by threat
of thought
                    —a rude toss of light—

rolling early manhood until the ledgers
kept at night are mirrored in my face:

the credit lies of facts   & the debit lines of choice.

Trackings₁

Highway 1 struggles North for the cliffs,
where black oak & coulter pines
shoulder light for the redwood.

Sea fog shifts in to Point Lobos,
to the gorges, lifts to split-pine
near this old cypress that gnarls
above Pacific—& I make for the wolf,

where the sea runs loud in my blood,
louder than the *"bee-loud glade,"*
where my love of deflection points
are caught between cypress & the eye:
this slippery syntax of my growth
       in geometric-West
in air with souls of dead Redmen.

Trackings₂

I gave up home the way a wall breaks down for rain.
Language is hard for a corner boy
in a city that stops at curbs.
A good lad knows his place, whether in Dublin or L.A.,
that back home is fallow,

where no one waves in a doorway,
where girls dance honored at the burials,
where mothers & fathers who look in mirrors
see their son's ghost walking down to Kilkeel.

I've learned to love off the road,
    & beneath,
how the bones of the dead sing in light,
how the wind blows through the barley.

the *break* of mariposa

is the blind crescendo of its color,
orange in opening like the soul
a husk to light—
delicate as wings. I was waiting
for transparent veins. Glass petals
                    breaking
in the Cities when I saw them in my boyhood,
saw their slash in sage, saw their
open stamens in tufted purple netting . . .
blooming in the Flagstaff snows a chiffon of mystery,
lenient against the mountains, tough, compelling,
                    a singe of beauty
& I felt

the dance of mariposa

in the foothills of *Califia*,
gold & shivering naked in the gulches,
a blush of grace in acoustic whispers
like wind-chimes cut from tin
in a serum cloud.

Tonight, I feel the wind around my throat,
& the mariposa-dancing flashes gifts
& hesitations, move vivid than the souls
who have gathered on this road.

And when they close their imaginations
to my ghost, I walk among their sleeping centers
with my urban shoulders,
& reach down to touch their
scattered seeds.

Spring lies

After nights alone in the Wigwam Hotel
I'm back on Rt. 66 driving to the
      CADILLAC RANCH IN TEXAS:
our Easter Island memorial to the millennium/

10,000 birds sing for the WEST while
the Maypole ribbons are black/
    & this road is full of gallowglasses—
heads shaved   cigarettes between teeth
and their hearts tent pegs driven in against
         winds/
On the Free-way organic lies look like facts
        for the human:

The rabbit white-out in snow/a Gypsy moth fade
on the birch/way that fawn quivers in fern

like this woman I see on a yellow park bench/
      under twin ELECTRIC GREEN TOWERS:
she bites into sandwich & stares at her shivering
           man
attenuated against his grey-sky of Texas
       silent & metallic/

Dark hands

at the *Balles Artes in Mexico City*—the dancers
choreographed the shooting when
    two drunk Frenchmen
stood up & sang their anthem.

Dark hands dragged them out.
I took the bus to see bullet holes at Puebla,
saw the cops in bars with rifles over shoulders
& beetles like polished amber.
                The empty golden domes of Spain

curve with blood &   *At some point*
you must trust the dark to do its proper work.
You must trust the muddy wall, the dirty map,
the old women with food & open doors,
Virgins & dead sons' photos on their walls.

Dark hands

further down to Acatlan, on a bus with men
in baggy white & machete-belted/
& at some point you forget the history/
rely on ways down from our huddled cities
to the spread of smaller places/shaded under ruins/
    I awoke before dawn, shivering,
&
    from the dark a dark hand provides *serape*.

I rolled up myself to Oaxacan walls
that loomed under the Zapotec sun/
        gave it back—

to the dark hand that lifted to Maximilian
before his last slow waltz with Carlota.

Stone lemons

The hike up steep from Oaxaca
& the sun a medallion where on hills
old *viejitas* build fires,
        small ones/flaming close to
            their living holes/
I remember the approach as strangers to ceremonies
cleft by the ghosts/& blood moving toward walls
in a cold breath of order/   High on that mountain
the stone mud pies of a god with their dead-feathered
        souls in the chambers like web
I remember the wind: heavy, carving-in the ruin/
moving in our clothes—then down into the open court
        and my White Heart contracts

To the click of anklets

It was the light in the cotton of her blouse
a blue-gold & covering her arms in chestnut
        darkening her eyes before Cortez
          & the slaughter of gold
No *corridos* only whisper of drums, of brown
feet in the dust & the feathered wind dancing
fanning into masonry into the clicks of her anklets.

The sun calls on Monte Albán & we carry the woven
mantas—We bend against walls of Zapotec stone *el danzante*
& sandunga winds spread the skirt into mystery
into stone flesh & clay blood—then my mouth into lemon
    into the shoulders of lemon
  her belt loosening the thick smell

Of Nahuatlan leather

holding in folds the blue cotton blouse
with its shaking embroidered flowers
      opening and closing/nestling
in the maize smell of clean market cloth.

She holds me against the engravings
against that carefully placed stone
      with its smell of the sun
& silver-cold are the stars of altar &
          knife
when she says: *"La brisa es mia."*

& now this is leathered in brain &
lemoned in body in the cold stone
      of lemon.

Of the warm equator

down from the green hills of Puerto Angel,
the village tiled roof & balconies shaded in leaves,
where at dawn in sea mist Roberto opened his cafe
to the *tewara* & *rumpope*, the pineapple & oranges.
The awakenings on shores like the long shadows of Voices
in waves, from the hammocks & rooms, the dank smell
of seaweed & rich sand—Utterances anywhere are of space,
women's tongues like the reeds, not like the stories we read.

And I heard not the hard, clank of steel ships
sailing away from their harbors, or the voices of warriors
fighting on decks, but fishermen in their singing,
stitching nets, dragging them to boats before the breakers
tossed time & their utterances around fires with good rum.
And then the light over me blue as the sea broke in their faces,
                              & took me back home.

Coming back

that night the call in my mother's voice,
folded on the phone . . . & I—

—breakdown-son—   lost to reform
shivering to the break like a bad actor said:
        "There's too much to be told."
When I arrive with paperbacks I greet her as Father
often stood—stewing clean his love—the way most
Irishmen stand at village dances: blank-eyed,
        —full of paid dreams unexpressed—
In his bedroom of sliding doors facing West
the windows open to the sea & Torrey pine,
& this pale light around his frame is *Califia* gold.

Father, hard lender, dying will increase the debt,
& slip my soul an iron mortgage.

To rooms

When I look upon the walls:
I see you in those photos: fly-boy in a B-52/the field
where you made Black troops inspect the shine of shoe/*&*
there: my sisters   me   in Sunday-clothes/
there: when you ran for mayor/odd-Republican in Irish green/
there: you & Goldwater reeling in the truth with swordfish/
& ME: dancing that night with Nixon's Virgin Daughter Trish,
HOWL and SONS AND LOVERS in my Chevy/

Gaelic stowage from Cork,
who brought the mail for New York Irish on 33rd.,
your forehead is the color of that yellow Lincoln
        /lodged in the garage/
the heap you traded in for the market-crash Ford.

His *blue eye*

For three days & nights I monitored the breathing,
felt the ankles, pressed fingers to the bone,
listened to the sea-murmurs mix with his . . .
& in this room where   the Eye
that narrowed when I used a masonry plumb
& leveled to the spread of mortar,
watched the putting down of brick,

the doctor said *"Slip the needle under skin
and wait."*

      It stayed fixed at center,
and when I slipped the needle that eye rolled in liquid blue
to fix me, plumb the word—then *flickered*.

Two fingers under breastbone for the *drum*.
a mortgaged rhythm to be unrhymed,
      a metaphorical cement in brick.

Heart Map

Dark roads that open out
    will look smooth
        when they lean in to woods,
            like the paths of genesis.

We are told they curve in hearts.

But things linear are lengths
        without the depth
        and measures cannot see

                the vanishing point

The design of a heart
        is that its everywhere

is everywhere

        equi-distant

from a   center

A Boy true,

running from the Loony Tune of Wall Street
& the radon-oedipal/in *this* language doomed
I wanted in the early mornings/o these
            —yellow trees that shake in memory—
                     dug out from scars in soft ruins/
I wanted the raw big hole in me/where even stars
are chained in blood/& tongues ripped out of bells.
I wanted to haul in the bundled wrappings/
I wanted to feel the loss of cloud
in the bastard caul of the road/
                          To hold out—
against the business . . . near the pines
in the backwash of emotion from April-grins.

A Boy tried,

as a lump on a stool in a cold sweat
for a hard roll & sour coffee/before the tickets & receipts:
ALL ABOARD for the 1-10 trip from Blythe to *Phoenix*.

Slow bus rides are for Outsiders. You know the ones:
the skull too small for the *Heap-Big-American-Dream*,
Redwing shoes too tight/& dirt caked on the collar.

I'm carried small on the vinyl seat,
& hear the squeak of rivets & lagscrews/
The Driver does not turn round in the

      economic butchery of it.
The display of cut meat on chrome.

Boy-heart

I climb in to the skin of worlds,
& the way up is steep on a two-lane road
   wild with boulders 6000ft.

I work to the silence of animal, & there is calm
through open windows. From my *given-point*
   I drive to the altitudes—
     where the yellow thighs of mountains
move their felt metamorphic-cores.
   I'm looking for *wild storage*, in Flagstaff,
& I roll down my window to check pulse.

Crags sharpened by frost, & the roots of *pinyon*
pry open rock. It is the mystery of silence
   in the *body*,
   as if I could be as old, as real,
      in my labor

to these snakes eyes,

   southeast on 66 gone
Freeway for the heat & seductive-SPACE
   until I see that stars hold
    light in their fists.
That under the eyehood of a rattler up State 10
   between sea & mountain
   my light-stripped memory
a thin silver beam in the creosote bush, to that
    YELLOW EYE
a needle point in brain at Red Rock under white firs
    above saguaros:
& the shade-hood of my lid closes to admit the road.

Odysseus in New Mexico

Out of the cities & past toll runs
        the highways flatten like seas—
I drove to the tiled roofs & deer paths,
where with wine I
        MADE RAID
on love in the backlands/with Penny
at her impossible LOOM/
& in my forest of memory the measure of distance
came flat-up through the steering . . .

O Red Roof of this world,
shelter me naked from Calypso/
        because this is my slow-burn on the asphalt/
with windows rolled up to the Sirens
        for a *scream*

The Southwest truth is here:
        a codeine of solitude
in the cargo of my bones/   so to the red-dusk gammadion
    of Arizona & dark turquoise-stone of New Mexico/
        my roads are
    the LOTUS-alibi—

for the desert is weathertight/& in the moonlit rattler's
        lidless eye,
in these mountains with their Aeolian dreams/the revolving

NAVAJO SWASTIKA

    The 800 blows of adulthood
        in the thundering amnesia of *Ogygia*

So with her

to that lemon rock of Tuscon/up stream in boot-splash
like convicts busted-out for air—/& the boulders
toys for gods/   We picked up stones like coins
& when we drove back down ORACLE we felt *darker*/

In Sonoran nights that took our breath/we heard the palominos
stomp their memories back to the Earth
                                under PICACHO
where the light we came to find

In yellow rooms

                        swirled like butter cream/
            & when we opened doors winds of hot-juniper/
    sheets folded back in gold/ Rooms like these contain secrets:
            this slip of limbs in emerald pools at the morning heat
                colors pale as rattler skin at night/

        I've come back to sleep in rooms with yellow light
                    to think of you
            crouching in your secret/how we leaned into the heat
                before we locked the door and left/

leaving New Mexico

and that bleeding honey-color
of round stone
smooth hoops
in the Navajo circle of birth

I've turned my back on the Gila Valley
on the Indian in his feathered breath
where the trade with skull for atom was made

PHALLIC CLOUD

burnt-orange in the teeth of Capital
your New Mexicans huddle in towns
on the edges of reflexive mountains
beneath our public History

If we sit in the Cliff Dweller's caves
above Silver City
behind a fire in those 700-yr-old rooms
we feel on those thin horizons of Arizona
the human need for

centering

like ponderosa
braced for the cold   for the floods

[In The Currents

What was that shaking, that low rumble?
I had gone to Klamath Lake for the shadows,
for the explanations, for the dark-roads
that open out in their heart-maps.
                    I changed tires in Yreka & waited
for the lying, the bravery.
                              I waited for
people in their breach of fear, the mouths I saw
buying car parts in Hawkinsville.
And I saw the holding of shoulders
                    in the Scott Bar mountains.

I wanted to understand the rite of pavements.
                    those currents driven green in that lake,
driven, in the shaking lumber trucks
                              rumbling down 263.]

Out Takes

I've always driven out of town,
out beyond the smell of bldgs. to pine.
I drive at night—as if to roll up on a road,
take it past L.A. & push it rough to Manhattan,
lift it from Phoenix & smelt it down in Chicago.
It's cheap. Just the price of gas. A gentle pressure of the foot
                    & the wind blows in a future through the window.

          American Roads are paved for the worker.
                    And you can leave things behind
                    in the cold-heat energy achieved by a dreamy
                    thermocouple.

Tonight, I'm driving out to Flatland—
                    my face lit up green by the dashboard,
and all this sound & light I feel are governed
          by the laws of Big Business.
                    Out my rolled down glass
are the *whispers of mountains*   who gossip about men.

Why not a nature-poem?

You want me to write a poem *au naturel*
                    because you are Romantics.
                              Imagine that.
You want me to be a poet. Write of:
cold mountains.   Navajos & pinyons.
See me hide in geology & salt tongue with seas.
See me hike to Palomar for galaxies & hunt
        for Orion's killing-star.

Well: I'm too tired to hike Rockies or trail wolf.
Too dizzy to dance with Hopi or go looking for
              WHALES
Too far from the L.A. decay & Hollywood Hills,
& I've ridden the monorail in our Weimar DisneyLand.

        So *you go imagine*
    imagine this: under the sulphur-cloud
    I hear the hum of 100 bundled men/
        I see the levi-feel of pleasure
in our lust of production/& in all those pinched faces incl. my
        own the thin-skinned Puritan-tantrum
        at even the suggestion of *beauty*,
                    or DEVI

Should I *sing*

the westernlands,
snapshot canyons in a postcard nightmare
and yowl to mountains,
                    listen for the sea in rail—
ache into *lyric* the self-conscious complaints
and idealize the redwood with an eye?

Or should I curse the green for you,
and look for those out-takes on a road—
all those alibis we use to make exits.

We expect this Earth to be lyrical.
We expect it to balance.
We want it to hold and to shoulder.

            To the lone and wheeling bird's
        eye to the sun. Become reptilian
        in green—

honing round the ocean's magnetic center
        and blinded by dusk;

To the naked claw,
        flying in the wings of blood and feather,
        tested in the winds to dip and plunge,
                as if they made their dreadful flight
                to nests in shadowed inlets:

To the restless birds, and to the necessary,
                to their chartless whisperings North—

I go—in the wing-rattled night,
            to the ancient murmurings,
                    booming outward for the riddled journey.

NORTH

North

Here. On the jump-off point for migrants,
down old truck farm roads to Chicago,
Lake Michigan breathes in her stumble
of ice. I see Northern-Lights
in the windows of an el. And here white mists
from the arctic wonders,   like bridal lace,
net hearts between buildings.   I turn

on East Grand, look at my face in the glass:
and out of the crowd it fuses.
Out of the crowd it marks its appearance, the sheen
of its forehead like marble under strobe light,
alone, temporary, loaded with visions that evaporate,
hot from a brain pan significant in love
and drifting on streets in a flood of departures.

Midstream

My fishing boot had plunged silver
        in the Klamath River
            & the fly line,
    anchored round a mossy log,
as if far more steady here in ripples.

The world did reflect there. Break up
        into sky chunks   cloud mirror
& all around the aspen down hard in yellow.

The only change was a *glint* of trout scale,
purple, clean, a smart rap on the surface.

There was tug before the fool of hook,
& drawn reel—
            more line than Kobayashi's dreams,

an arc that bends from Paterson to Seattle.

        Where nothing in between is balanced.

Last Look

Don't get me wrong. I'm not complaining.
It's not the way streams roll blue around my thigh
              and chill the shoulders.
       Or the way our roads serve up
                        the vertical cities.

It's just that   *haiku is impossible in America*
                        there's too much to say.

I stopped for the last look
just this side of Denver on State 70, Clear Creek.
The road North still cut near a mesa—

[where I left you standing by the horses
saddled down for the moons]—   one road:
                        a clear trail back to ponderosa

the other: this present long drive up cement,
         my face green in the *mirror*.

Struck once

the Pleasure Boat explodes on the Ohio,
and the factory owner, wife and son
fade under the oily wake.
Local 325 on strike but heard the sound
from the line—splinters, sail, deck
cascaded down in black smoke.
Men on the line ate fried fish fixed
by their wives that day, and along the banks
of the Ohio people were seen foraging:
grey clay yields the salvage, things to sell,
to barter—cushions, new mast, redwood planks
all sold for food by the "bankers"
while 325 waited for the assumption of
                    power,

waited for new pay,

and Luther Jameson, wife and son
floated slowly and secretly down
          the Muddy Ohio,
And Black men caught fat catfish,
small food for their night in the Midwest,
in the old, brick buildings of the Midwest
          one hundred years old
sinking in to the clay   sinking in to
          the warm, historical,
                    Ohio soil.

And as I lifted my canoe from the White River,
there snagged in the limbs of a fallen maple
          the body of Luther,
his diamond ring glistening in the September sun.

Circumference

Driven from the WEST
        to this air *webbed* with memory/
            to this disturbance of
      your BALANCE
found in girlhood to the eyes of a Father—
& now to a safer lover

I came nude like a cloud
        heavy with clock/
& you first did the charm & swagger when you took risk
          & asked who was I

in the hay-smell of your bedroom,
           its windows open to the rain—
the flood-biblical so difficult
        in the modern brain
yet forgiven at the gas stop
            before my EXIT EAST &
        your tariff /

      Would you know your own smile
          in my circumference?
Would you know the geography of my arms?

When I bend into you like a wave
        returning to its ancient form,
Would you let me see you as a bird?

Could you come to the ROAD of energy
        in some extravagance
          and tell all in the *I should say* as your
unreasonable passions   & DEVI?

Steeltown Love

From the blue of sea and roar
of its waters, it is now only ghosts-faces,
memories of the sea-damp smell at night.
I'm living farther North, where men pull up
their collars to Canadian winds.

I shall not die West. This great lake has me
in its grip, and the smell of steel is deeper than the brine.
The sky a polished enamel, and the sun must
tear its way through cloud. All along the shores
Northern lovers are walking icy-hot in coats,
their nipples hard and lips blue with speech.

I know the loneliness of that lake. I know
its whispers. Its secrets more primeval than the sea.
And far on its horizon the spectacle of a city,
packed with moaning buildings and lovers' glances.
The ice shelf cracks and gives—
the way my Northern love falls from anger.

So tear me open when I reach for you.
Grip me with your open legs on this moving dune.
Kiss the sea from my mouth, and show me
the blue of your Northern eyes. Give it hard,
like those waves on their granite quarries,
and pull me male to your steeltown shoulders.

Roads red & east

My *body* on these pages
turned on the Midnight Roadway—
        the U.S.A. frisk rolled out at night.

On roads from oceans to the midwest dilemmas,
where millhands bash windshields with bats
        to see glass shatter like stars:

Arapaho souls slither in the dreams of Frank Lloyd
        & dance on the Mounds of Ohio.
They chop down the totems of Manhattan
        & bang chains in the hulls of San Diego.

The road north is liquid-red
        & the explanations I hear
make angelic sense in the death-holes of our history books.

To the grey suits in their Rotunda
        I step alone
to the lake waves, to the steel mills on dunes,
        to the shouts in clapboard houses
huddled under the smoke of machinery.

Escape

Difficult to complain without the finger-modern
calling dark critique the rouse of self-pity.
I'm radical, searching for insurance against
lacerations,   for those
              under the floorboards of the Castle who
still find in their nouns a dream—I wait—
         to be released in the thunder.

I see the dance to the neighborhood pyre of roses,
& along our spines the language of *sleep* & spookulations:

the SS-laughter of the shoe salesman/the superego of Telephone/
the phantom mothering of our TV/the supercooled offramp
& soft array of boxed goods/the zombies of maquiladores
the movie screen breast & our—caskets as beds—/

[Red Angels

in my veins, you moved in under-love
& I emerged lashed in freedom to the ignorant hills.

There is no blame in emergence,
in my quiet maneuver you
listened to my oaths & my lies—

              Until finally,
filling up the Chevy with global gasoline
              I broke through those borders to Chihuahua

         & drove headlong to Zacatecas for the stones
                        & their whispers,
& to Puebla   where Maximilian slow-waltzed before being
                        shoved up to the wall]

Milltown

Tonight, in my gritty milltown's ease,
I look to the lights on the Amoco refinery and ask
if New Mexico boulders are real in their gentle pink soils.
If those stalking red mountains
       still reach up to a moon.

Walk once
       to the winds off these dunes
and you hear in the cold artic-voice of Chincoteague
       our breath of seas in the *marram*.

Fix your vision of lovers,
       piled up in cities
          scrambling over stone.

Scratch surfaces anywhere
       and you find the split skull of Indian,
          a bit of rag over bone
          a ring on a fossil-knuckle,

like the things we bury in each other
       under the el

like our *words*   in Amerika's *sleep*.

Beach North

Lake Michigan stays clean around its edges.
No ghosts of *Conquistadores* or sharks.
No roiling of whales. When you sail-out beyond USX
                      you feel *depths*,
      and you know
this lake can down freighters, swallow families.

If you swim, you feel the cut
of slim surfaces, ordorless and primitive.
If you dive, you see pig iron, iron bars,
      and clean shipwrecks.
If you dig, you find only the smallest of shells,
as if Nature had made a clean sweep of grandeur
      and settled out of court.

If you love,   in the dunes
you look for the long path that won't
plunge too intensely to wild roses,
for the sand cherry that fades in the summer.
And you use the theology of Carnegie
to bathe real desire in the acid of amnesia.

All over your landscape are the clues to your feelings:
the deadly whispers from surf, cold winds from the North
and low *thump* of the mill. For this is the land
that bends to a beautiful stubble, and the compound
of your heart your reservation protected by daydreams.
This is the place where that Magical Adam we no longer know
walks to his Invisible Eve, in the old, turgid darkness
                  and condemned beauty of desires.

Down from Winnetka

It's getting late
& the street lamps are blooming like lilies,
their poles look officially straight.
I've put my arm around your waist,
and we know that men
have pulled up their collars to *mist*—
they dissolve through the revolving glass doors
of these buildings that exhale their dreams.

So down from the canals & gas works
of Whiting, down from the Kirk Yards to beaches
the mills ring in thunder for the dunes,
for the midnight-men who live in the smoke
& mutter in 10,000 hot rooms.

Lake Michigan sits calm for a ship, or a death,
             & my
        OZ-Chicago
floating like a casino, uptight town
sloped-shouldered to the Banks,
you stay fixed in your homage to our faces,
waiting in our trucks for the green.

Mill Bar

I know street lights at midnight
are lit up for the sleepless/
because we broke out & looked at our hands
in the amber before walking through doors/
& when that smoky pool room lit you up
the pool cues struck home
     the only thing left for our pockets:
  soft thefts in a bar
where others come in for their dreams
    in the U-TURN of their faces/

There is this smell of wet wood in a mill bar,
as if the soakings could never be mopped/
And when I watched you listen to your friend's
   talk of sleepwalk
     your body edged up to mine
where tender lies are the truths/
     where things take us by surprise,

And you said,

"Last night I woke up & felt chains
    in my skin/
so looked deep to find gravity in my bones—
    how they tilt South—to the horses/

    See these maps around my mouth?
   they point to that *center* he can't find.
And the half of me that tilts South
still rings! while the other sheds light on the ice"/

Orange quarters

And I said: If you look out that subversive window
you will see that moon-hammer summer come
        down in Lake County/
& the smell of lake-water you've known since your
girlhood in this strange light of Portage pounds down
like comfort. That light so yellow   a metallic cloud
blooming from the gas works . . . /

     —boiling up like a bomb—

and through the walls you can hear flint-screech of boxcar,
rusted chassis at stop signs/& the yell of drunken hillers
    off the nightshift from INLAND STEEL
      But when you clanged your gold leg around my thigh bone
didn't we do it up right?/   until your mind knocked out its duties,
punched me back to those roads where trucks like graceful *hearses*
                  squeezed me to an EXIT for a drink/

   where the fog of Whiting smells like gas/
                   & the light off Lake Michigan
        shivers orange on the jukebox quarters in my pocket/

Old Wisdom

[Well, she said, I said]. I still drive one-way streets
as if there were some city plan for such roads/
    After Boston grids became popular—
             slicing land into SQUARES.

We like such order/   it helps us to
fortify our truths: *the courthouse   the jail   a bar*

When I drive in Chicago all the one-ways seem
to fade into neighborhoods/& the more I try for
        Tom's Mill Pub
the longer I drive by the banks & neat quiet homes—
    those solid structures with such *curb appeal.*

        Since Babylon we've
known such happy routes/they bring us to where
        Big Business says we should BE/

      Yet there is such comfort in the wildness of dusty roads,
          where two-way humans
break free for single moments   shouting drunk in love!
         with their mountain-towns.

Love unemployed

ROY ORBISON is hitchhiking on the turnpike
& his *tremolo* no one can find/
so that flat, these ROADS—the burn of memory—
        the slot machine of TIME USA
with a PATSY CLINE death & the thunder of Beethoven on
        the Freeway.

O the way D.H. Lawrence sought *equilibrium*
        with a lung gone frothy & his love-in-a-dell/but now it's

love laid off & no money back/& I'm   routed out
with a pitchfork from the Barn & no profitable redemption/

why it's *you*—in your shaking deliveries!—
The rocked womb in its Virginia Reel/electric in storms,
& we dance in the marathon before *"they shoot horses,"*
before movings blown in pines take down the houses!

lover in a milltown

Smokestacks
hold me liable
in the burn and
majesty of service.
I watch them
give off what wives
call grace of labor—
     oxides
turning snow
the color of oranges,
the sun to Mars.

Chicago floats like OZ.
The John Hancock in a cloud.
At dusk the sky stretches red to Gary
and the flames of gas flues
wave so strangely above the ghettos—
where men with broken English drink in bars,
their faces thick with lead dust,
their eyes like lanterns.

This smell of metal
for the children who play at sundown,
who shout like being murdered
by something going on
inside them:
(their fathers waiting in the clapboard kitchens,
their mothers stewing meat.)

At night, just above the bogs and wetlands
along the shores of Ogden Dunes,
     that red parabola
that burning halo which keeps me here.
A burn of oaths in furnaces.

Hold me, milltown woman.
Athene in jeans.
I hear the wheels tonight.
Ezekiel's wheels.
The low groan of mills
throbs in our bedroom wall.

Coming back

with a bus-growl from O'Hare,
back from *Califia* to Chicago

there comes the memory of my mother
        whispering at the picture window
framed by the sea—that blue which
            plugged the Westward-Ho
            & brought up short our dreams:
one by one she picks up shells
        kept high on a shelf
turns them over with her fingers
        peering at them
to discover in their curves
        the answers
she cleans them, blows dust from the dried starfish
            & gazes at the blue-whipped waves—

When I left, the salt-crushing air
        hung in beads on the jacaranda,
            & from the cabin
        I saw the black waters
of San Diego lit up by a flaming car crash.

Tonight, before my connection to New York,
        I see tired faces loaded
down with the usual souvenirs
        from those warmer prisons of our world.

And as we rocked into Hammond,
            I could see
        lead-dust crusting on the icy windshield of my car

and one lone Black man   limping

who must have shadow-boxed his way
        from Broadway   where I saw him last.

Southern detour!

Selected Amerikan random for *Millennium* Car Race
in a hick dump down Rebel South
this yell given like boys of Gettysburg to the post
gets the YES!/   Come on redneck peckerwood
with yr. wallet chained to pocket!
Your Chevy Babe waits with her Playboy knockers
shoved out in the denim of her country!
A Georgia peach so keen on being picked/before
a Black chick rubs up against yr. grey-boy leg
& brings down the Tennessee State Rotunda!/

This checkered patriotism of White/Black,
& on humid nights the *mixin'* behind barns
so old the courtrooms cannot stand it/Hear Yippee!
as if the ethic of BIG COCK AMERIKA in a backwater
swamp is all *gone with the wind* in magnolias . . .
& Lee is seen shopping for a lawn mower
with his Wal-Mart credit card.

Skin Diving

Given the chains on sea bottoms in Spanish harbors
it's 9pm in Chicagoland/& no matter how we talk
blue shackles of this city fit so calmly under our
bagpipe cloud & squeal of bird/like steel Xmas
eternal & time that size of dime from birth to death/
shoved in a pocket for the toll & o it's am delivery alright!/
like a milkman with his bottled love evaped! on a front porch,
& over head after zip! out cubicle the belly of a sea gull like a bomb
from ZEUS/Even breath smells like rust in a room where judges
pass out, get their wrists patted by a beauty queen temp with points
for good sport/& the rabbi who pokes his head from under a
                    TROOPER
sees Ezekiel's Wheels spinning on Chicago/7pm in Tucson & the
Wheels there spin over the Galiuro Mts./& o stuff the last-time
zodiac food in my mouth to speak of no one in the east or west
deserving of a delivery/I've given it all to the warm sea-bottomed
chains & there wave like a dead sailor whose lips have kissed
the mechanical mermaid for 1,000 yrs./& all this required just
to walk by the clubs of hell on Clark: rocking in their wheels.

Baud-sonnets

I drive out at night as usual in the tensile mist,
To speed & let air brush out the thought.
My head breaking & I cannot find my breath
In hope—caught up in worlds once
Large enough but now with padded walls—that
Move in an oily noise   a tuned-in direction:

[SPACE seems smaller in this age]

A concrete esplanade with posted guards along the meadows,
Where nothing can be heard but   *beating silence.*

Blinded lovers are bused to the thickening rooms
Where Kafka spoke   in dreadful eloquence.
And there: my gutted name a ghost that walks.

Mouths are plugged with cotton & brains electrified,
Our simple loves & actions called a *simple crime.*

And then you come dancing through the fog!
Static & complete. O Electric Lover!
Disk of touch & hard drive word & tongue,
Tapping window access with ginger-Press-Command!
My *ping*! of start-up paper jam & ragged right.
RETURN Right-justify. Scroll & Set **shadow** -print!

CRT moonlight-**bold** in desire *controlled*
A gogo-to & highlight boilerplate   block retold

In ancient song & document dump! sublime!!
Encoded now   in fixed-point arithmetic:
A memory cycle of composite character   on-line.
To chip of protocol & parity bit—*I am synchronous.*

Impact character! Printhead body & program mind!
I *queue* for you. For menu. *Click!* for view mode:
ENTER

55

Horizontal

The soft thud of something permanent in the horizontal—
the way things fall & stretch, go down warm & unafraid
in farewell, & singing in the grasses to metallic latitude.

The distance-equidistant from points in discovered curvings
migrate from a road. Line by line I'm simplified
in the flesh, and do not need the commandments of a couplet.

Put your ear to Earth for the dark-electrical in surface & under,
the alien-astral, eye-level to horizons with your lips so close
to the dangerous cores—the body found & dumbfoundedwidth.

Take the road & curve it down from the iron perpendicular.
Shape it in the longitude of darkness with a foothold in the demiurge.
Accept it male & female in the god-born-horizontal.

Give me the weight of base. Give me the architecture of nothing
but the curving-line. The sweepings. Let me fall & stretch,
go down warm & unafraid singing in my riches to the metallic.

HORIZONTAL

vertical

Under the shadow of buildings in vertical
men walk sleeping in dreams,
the soles of their feet picking up stardust,
their breath in the night.
Men with glass souls tangled in doorways,
trousered in cloth stamped with inspections,
their faces like porcelain.

How do we know of their steps,
or the depth of their sight?
How do we stitch theory and practice
from the pulpits and boardrooms
and soothe them with stories,
retold in our technical kindness?

I'm glad I have eyes for the night
when the illogical cloud moves in for the kill,
and disguises each death with a dangerous kiss.

I'm glad I can see the material of heaven,
in its close-fitting cloth for the Earth.

Lake Michigan

I keep returning to this lake
to walk the long shore
to listen to ships.

To the cold
I can't help thinking of *beams*,

riveted with words,
verbs for a frame
of certitude.

Chicago sways in steel
the way the brain rocks in dreams,
and in all those Gothic rooms

where prayers are said,
the dark bells still announce
the deliveries, the payments,
the profits.

I work in this lake-light,
riveting words
before they are spoken,
and I keep blueprint for
the ghosts of repairmen.

Tonight
I look out over the cobalt blue-waters
and speak—
under the lights of the Amoco refinery,

and I ask if I am entitled to love
in these winds, that shake steel.

Edge sideways Athena, because

I'm here, on the edges, for your trip
in the MIDDLE/   I surround you
with sound of sea & rock/You can look in your mirror
& brag, with *this me*/no matter how you feel abandoned,
ignored by the shifts of Wall St. & the Fathers/
You are athletic! Atmospheric! Lonely for a ROOM
of your own/   o come here even to a milltown, lover!
Where in the girlhood of your steel-making shields
the Aegean vernacular murmurs in the locomotive!
Break through the trees where I camp in the elms,
by Bethlehem Steel/& in the Dunelands
you will disturb these thighs of men/grown silver
in their working-class chrome/   asking for the fire of Olympus!
Take me like you see me! Waiting in the bad company of my bones!

Weather report[1]

People here tell me to bite the free bullet,
go throw myself up, pace out the steps & behave,
take my godawful mouth out of sight & buckle it shut—
the way I saw father put on his sales-face for others
& ship off his *likelihood* to the Shakespearean suburb,
the way my sister burned to death in her room
when she stuffed love in a drawer & all night tried on dresses.

It's the way people look: pale-Americo behind a set lip,
sitting in Cheshire-mouths like a load of bitterness.
Shake hands, & you feel that flat danger of armed woodsmen
who haven't seen women for a year, a round eye that gives you
            the once over.
Talk & it doesn't take much to stir up the prognosis:
a whole shelf of tears just waiting to collapse
& that dull seething in a forehead stuffed in fists,
tight-ready to smack beauty in the mouth.

I've got all those expressions that frighten the locals,
threats of rebellion as old laughter in Temples.
I've got this bald passion too rank for the Midwest,
a prayer shawl of blood & skull cap of noise,
& I want the all loose & the woolly, the uprooted dilemmas,
the baggy voluptuousness of a secure woman
who isn't afraid to make *gestures* or publicly say:
"Write me full & write me beautiful!"

Modern Air

USA Flight 333 to New York
& the pilot comes on & says:
>   *"Hey folks, if you look to your left*
>   *you'll see the Northern Lights."*

—and there—
just a faint blue-grey haze.
Hardly enough for an announcement.

But the pilot kindly dipped Wing
& the whole crowd ducked its head to look . . .

no *"Ooo's"* no *"Ahhh's"*

Just a quiet *ho-hum*.
As if we expected no luck
at seeing the alien lavender,
as if we could no longer see
non-ethical splendor.

Pilots do their best to hold our hands.
They know the mysteries of concealment
& they soothe our resignations,
secure our movements through the modern cloud
that veils our true colors:

pale truth of bone & placenta-blue—

10,000 feet up.

Migrant Progress

NOW   toward ENDings
                    before millenniums bring us up
                                      & I'm walking
in NY   city still smoking from its bldgs.
                    I hear a roar in my-Midtown-light.

          This is the month for bundling up,
& the TUBE   is pointed North for *progress*
          in this *"best of all possible . . . "*

                    {to the boyhood on beaches
seeing molecules!/father in his big business suit
stepping-out like Harry Truman/my sisters in their
star-lit dresses coming home from men & smelling
moonlit-jasmine/   & twitching silver mother-eye
                    snapping off lights/
and me: with my bags to Arizona—my rumble to Oaxaca—
my ferry to Vancouver & cruise ship to Alaska—my hitchhike
to Kentucky & bus ride to Missouri—my sojourn in Ohio &-back-
flip-to-Califia—with 66 to Chicago—& stumble to New York:

this shaking girl in brownstone-walkup where her father
          meets me at the door & whispers horizontal

"We're now at our grindstones, sharpening our pens and blades,
taking all the rolls and clubbing others safe.

We've taken all precautions, laced up the grudging agreements,
divvied out the clothes and beefed up the public defenses.

And those who raise objections to the art of our duress,
are fed the proven distractions and laughed at in the press.

For no one has a second thought at playing the issued tunes,
and if a note is dropped, there isn't a reasonable excuse.

The wisdom of the few, rings empty in our common ear,
and for our sloppy soup we accept the kindly terror.

So flee to the borders, quick! if you have nothing to lose,
for the rest of us will emerge in comfort to abuse."

So White collar goes to heaven

on Broadway at am/
where the hitchhikers still raise thumbs to drivers
who think SCORE—office-donkeys
lugging prayers in a cowskin briefcase
& emerging from Chevy dripping flame/
with their noses pointed NORTH—

souls under the *clamp*   of lid-TUPPERWARE-U.S.
puffed-down so tight in clothes they still feel
touch of dove in human lip all gone to heaven on 32cd./
where the WRECKING BALL has taken down
the walls & pressed them to the rubble of their poems/

My optic nerve too sore now for the sight of kiss/
where the road curves round the dredging
up of oily rag & fender/up love in a pewter jar with paper roses
on a desk & ten full packs of sugar
opened 1 by 1
stirred in with geometric finger—
& I think: just *one* more el-ride
for those PLUMS
before the lid pulled down to neon/

Cannibal review

It's always Broadway slugged up in the face.
The Times Square fibrillations that have us trapped.
A whole gulp of profit like wolfing down a meal on the Donner,
as if eating hearts boiled up on the sidewalks.

There's always something in the looks we get—
as if we've just stolen plastic angels from a dime store.
You know, the ones people stick on their dashboards for Brooklyn.
Hung by its wings on a rear view mirror
to keep away the dripping tooth—
the ones that turn green when you turn off lights in a bedroom.

It's true. *Wild men roam the streets eating angels.*
They sit down at lunch & pull them wiggling out of pockets,
and no one dares to see if they are real.

Men eat them raw, or cooked up in the privacy of their kitchens.
They feed them to their guests in *hors d'oeuvres* before deals,
until the fat boys bloated with approval float above 5th Ave.
        like a Macy's Day Nightmare
roped down & held by the ticker tape ghost of Geronimo.

No account in New York

No amount of middle-class disinfectant
could stop the bad smell.
The absolute clean speed of America
on the brink of sale in NY.

Like polished chrome
the baldness of a banker's head & the pristine headlamp of a
      Lincoln.
It's Tom Jefferson with his soft little black girl
behind the Tidewater shed/& Franklin pinching the buttocks of
      Paris.
Whoopee!   *& How do you do you!*
& the beggars on Wall divvy up the umbrellas
as soon as you exit hotel & hail cabs to the Bronx.

Oh, yeah. It's the big Manhattan come-on. A jerk-off of gold.
The subways slick with nightmares & the brownstone kick in
      the groin.
All those furs from the hair of Indian/
        & the nipple ring clipped on in the alley/
    until the Club-Jazz offers you lead weight
      in the stone of your throat,
& the only thing that makes sense is a *skyscraper of pine*.

Mule Song

Long tall in the saddle & eager
meshuga-me in the fluid of my homeland:
skinny-chested-proper-bowlegged with a mother's support
i'm launched i'm set off i'm Texas free in a two-bag popcorn movie/
big roundup bar mitzvah down a stoned street in Yonkers
this brown-eyed Soho Cowboy to the peel of cloud & cobalt blue
in the Queens-Midtown Tunnel i'm *immaculate* in cast iron
thinking discarded grass in subway & tipped boots
in the Flower Market/i'm washing hands in City College come
too abstract for a chrome blower & o to be a lone buckaroo!
getting a haircut, standing like a cactus at a WALK light with
wind-rush of taxi a choke of thought/& heap big love cube on my
            withers
shagging with the staggers i'm buying a Xmas throatlatch
at Lord & Taylor for a lope in Highbride Park at pm & o how
sundown-takes-its-red from Phoenix in an ashcan! a stuffed down
glow so pandemic in the Midtown blowout that we ride in the flux
& fluid of a full-hipped sidewalk to Tribeca for one long tall
look down a penny paper want ad & beer thrown back
for luck.

Gestapo Sandwich

His words were the police before he jumped from the bridge.
And his brain read like a sitcom canceled from boredom.
If you remove it & slice you will find in its folds
a hero who bites bread with a Nazi
& shoves his soul into a boxcar to Mars.

He ate pickles before he plunged up to his neck in the Passaic.
A full stomach is better than being jacked-off in a cab.
There's only one way to see this:
he could no longer lift his legs out of bed,
or shove the brush in his mouth. The leather belt
he wore to the Deli was bought for meat by the waiter,
& he was rolled for his boots by the hobnail love of a jailer.

O how could he walk naked in New York to the Village,
or hitch back to Ohio. The rabbis have it all figured out:
it's Jonah-food for the slob & a boil for the coward.
And the lover will always demand truths from a tongue.

In Paris the SS sips tea with accountants,
& the sandwiches served up smell like the defecation of bats.
He flies out from the rail—glides home like a stone.
Unnoticed by tugs pulling in the Queen Mary.

Hanging coffins

I can't reassemble my puzzles so let me hang
like the coffins of Yangste. Tucked into granite
the way a Monarch wing is slipped into its envelope.
It took me years to haul myself up with ropes,
to let the workers wedge me in.
I lie down with the smell of pine & mined salt,
& the *Tao* is recited at sunrise before the masked dance.

I'm sleeping. I'm dreaming as fast as I can.
I'm waiting for players to exhume me, with my mind
still intact, & when they open the lid the odor of butterfly—
a sandalwood breeze through the clover, & the light
from those mountains glimmers here in the taxis on 58th.

O brownstones, the trifecta of death shall pay off in fixed races,
& the winding sheets we toss off will float over Manhattan.
I can walk dead in my land & still hear the bells of Peking
4000 years old as they bang deliberately with ghosts.

And if you can't see me then don't bother to look. Because
I like the invisibility of men who come back from the puzzles.
I like the invisibility of women who refuse to look up the answers,
people who disappear in the breach.

Love all bushed

So we go down blazing with our double-barreled souls
pointed at the moon, & we ache for one last night in the yellow—
the way we knew roses in the junk-talk of the world
too pale & silly for the wet winds off Lake Michigan.
O you had it set right in your teeth. You knew the tongue,
the take-off clothes in the art of modern-love, & make a man hard
& ready for a wallop, with his smart-mouth brainless like a flower
& his two big hands gone over to you in the amen of it:
this down between crazy legs that rice cake too hot for roses,
a banquet on a trail, washed out by those boiled rains
come down from skies too wide for beauty, & too busy for back-talk.
O I had it set right in my ribs with a god-finger probing home
& me carried bald in protest to the mercy of it, until the floorboards
gave way & the tumble sounded like a bass note from an angel
drunk on jealousy, whispering secrets no one should ever hear.

Love all bushed—in the last big act, & we stomp the boards
like those square dancers in *Oklahoma!* with their hands behind their
          backs
& a corn beam in their face. I've got on my hat for the roundup,
you've slipped on boots as pissed as Athena in a godless theatre &
the kettle is on the stove. So never mind the would be & rattlesnake
          of hope:
love all bushed—flushed & finished like a pacer losing big at Churchill.

Let's smash it in the mouth before it calls a broker,
& take back what was stolen in the hum of washers bolted to a
          basement.
In the clean cool sheets put on at night the swaddling of our solitude,
for the hot brain on its pillow is proud in the misdemeanor of its
          dreams.
So let's go down blazing with those warrants in our pockets,
& in our skin we'll rhyme it for a garden plowed up at night.

Weather report₂

I can't feel anymore the clubbing of money,
the old switch & bait or the cannibal eating my eyes,
the-o-come-over-here-&-give-me-your-throat-or
give-me-your-hands-for-the-gloves-issued at night.
I can't taste the candy words of our Weather
shoved in my mouth, sold to me retail by the brokers of OZ.
The Kindheads who come knocking with their unflappable take.
The boom & bust of my valves from the floodgates opened by
                gnomes.
The circus is broke, & the animals are talking, sworn in then stewed
                good
in their juices. 10 waves are over the sea wall & our flesh is all wet,
& the sleeping bags we tuck in the corner are dragged out at noon.

I am the *atomic lebensborn*, & in the cilia of my lungs
this strontium-90 of Xmas the relaxation of soup ladled out to the
                strikers.
O I know I'm ungrateful. Never crossed the Donner Pass of Chicago
& offered my leg for the pot. Accepted food hungry from a Navajo
                who smiled.
Got *serape* when cold in Oaxaca from an Aztec who wore machete,
even picked up by a Baptist who told me a tale of seduction.
It's just that I don't know what to do with my funk-love—
when these weather reports are made daily on the state of my fungus.

So go. Go say what you want about HOME & our borrowed-up sex.
The interest rates are no longer shocking & it's swallow yourself
                whole on installments.
The compounded daily forgiveness is forgotten when it rains in your
                head,
& the cost of construction rolls eyeballs in fatigue at the height of the
                Wall.
My dear U.S.A., getting kissed in the dark is expensive, & the rest
                sends you packing.
So don't tell me about *temperatures*, & don't lie about spring.
I've heard all the excuses, & we know your sweet-talk & jives.

O USA! USA my love, I'll make do with your dole!
Just leave me a few scraps to cook on my own.

bumming₁

and driven horizontal from *Califia* to New York along the WHITE LINE
of me-migrant-imago
taken to the pulse of our hard grateful sights
lined up by the road/
a display of CUT METAL
& soft toys in the cold iron-shadows of boardwalks—
where you dip in WARM WATERS with suns rising in the orange
of strange weather/

Under skin-bloom in filaments of muscle it is the
ASPHALT OF PRESSURE
& close-weight edged *in* to my bone/
the best way in a throat once whispering in its childhood
to the seas
but now stardust felt only off roads
in the night of blue *HORSE*
&

bumming₂

in living thick-late as humid-sax in old Dixie wet with magnolia
tasted in mouth/
a-long-held-out-note-absorbed-by-my-crushes-to-things- viscid &
congealed in the slo-mo-roll of hot COMEBACK from the winters
of E^b anemia/
to the notes in their C-major chord of PEACHES ripe between knees
& made for the jam

a bitter marmalade so sweet in this smoke
that it takes smooth run-up inside & round *plexus*
for need/
a plumb-down to a bottom full of registers where
warmth rumbles in meadows

& THERE . . .
no one to dispute the harmonics or tempos

when they hold . . . when they fold . . .

to the orchestral thighs of ATHENA.

Western problems

These round trips are always   ONE WAY
A waltz in a dance hall with one hand on your suitcase
& the other checking wallet . . . schmaltz with a PARKING METER
& the good tick of *doom*/Good Soldier Schweik in the bottom
of K's Castle & mobile Sancho Panza with his Don in a Chevy
on the FREEway

                    & o that western youthful heart has its adolescence
STUCK in boots/levis & T-shirt in a good Brando Pose:
half-queer & sado-hetero in the shank button of Wall St.—
A problem of philosophy with too much SPACE for a rabbinical
          footnote
& no additives in the soup of Manhattan/

                    when all we have to do is stoke
up in our rooms for nirvana in a car-crash of PARKS
& try not to submit for inspection/   so that

under the metallic cloud WE appear Whitman electrified to kiss
Rousseau-dreams/with one eye on the COKE-can left on the moon.

SO TAKE this day in the U.S. Take the bottom line.
              O you know the actuarials/the estrangements/
      the working hands & those minds
              that built the ice cream of Las Vegas
                        & spread out the reservations/

You know the Bronx & the vibrating *barrios/*
              the way Disney's Land is built on a swamp of blood/
              the way Wall Street rattles our cages/

You know who sits in the Friday night bars & those who eat out of cans
                        under bridges/

Because you've heard DIXIE sung & the anthem of Oil/
Because you've seen the FreeWays loaded with slaves/
        Because you're coming up for air!
                    while the LORDS OF CAPITAL are asleep
              in their Castles/

Road Signs

1
Now if you see me you would see me
      curving in a middle
         here or there
      between the redwood
& sea, between this lake & the *marram*.

    ROADS OPEN   like borderlands

for a moment,   as if I
         ignore the ENTRIES & EXITS.

Heart maps are folded into hills,
      lit up at dawn
      & in rooms I am *migrant*
    disentangled from knottings
      & the tenor of betrayal

    SOUTH OR NORTH to my

           vanishing point

The product of my gaze is

    HORIZONTAL

    a little triumph over social

    | —a tunneling under memory— |

on a road where at turns
    the irony of *agave!*

I've come down on my doom
of saddlecloth in these yellow winds that are
        RADICAL
and I wait for the Ghost Dancings/for the bones
of ages lacquered in their sandstone/

       & my eyes to you are lit by the campfires
where we are
       under pine with our knees in the *ajo-lilies*,
where we need Milky Ways.

2
To the pale Catalinas
       the sun rises sharp in a desert—
and the movings of *Cañada del Oro* are silent/

This morning is cold for the *cholla*,
and doves weave their transparent nests
       under MOUNTAINS

From Oracle, where *columbines* point to gulches/
       to the blazing *mariposa*

  this terrifying balance between

       FLOWER & STONE

& under the glyphs of MT Lemmon
       we camp like *sacahuista* on the Rillito
       and wait—

  10,000 clicks! From 10,000 waving plants!
       in silence

until the sunrise tightens love to that yellow dome
       & we spread the red-weaved blanket

       to our shift of sockets
       to a core of thickness

faces *West*

> Back down now from the smoke
> in a dream of REDWOOD I wonder how
> pith shall grow out rings in Mendocino/
> the argument has been made for *paradise*—
> I made it in a drugstore up Halsted in Chicago
> where I took it like Hui Shan on the Pacific
> who first saw the *palo colorado*

> so filmic & fresh

> There's a slide show on Broadway from NY to Seattle—
> & it's 1,000,000 yrs. old & Taxodiaceae primitive/

> *The redwood*
> buds male/female
> from branches picked up 1st by the Spaniards:
> (*madera* in the blood-red mind of gold)
> named by an Austrian *sequoia* after crippled Cherokee
> who wouldn't know his White Father—
> while Mokelumne called it *wawona* & drank its sap
> for a hope of mystic powers/
> & the whole BIG SHOW mistaken for a newsreel
> (when the Brits called it *Wellingtonia*)

> Now *sempervirens* in the Shangri-la of STATE
> mistaken for the metaphor of power
> /cut/
> down to build a thousand shacks for miners who will work
> backstage at the MET—trained as *ushers*
> with their flashlights beaming in our faces
> for GONE WITH a Wind

> The Feds *know* what counts in the symbol of supply
> & send men for the silent logging
> while Tokyo shims its panels
> before the BOMB   a light that burns
> our TAO love-positions at dawn

> & the plum blossoms drop cold
> in the harbor of DR. NO

In fog-floes the redwoods survive
like salesman with tight shoes/roots deep in
                    the Coast Range of
          CRAZY MOUNTAIN
                    where under the billboard EYEBALL
of EASTWOOD/
                    (toothpick in his teeth
                    with that smile of death

a stone-cold Drifter   /& peninsular bandit/
     protector of Marin from the Czar's nursery-seed—)
                    it was Wales
with its Caliban that claimed the transplanted
                    GARDEN
          a SUPER-Star world/

Facing West—
in the way it took hold on the planet:
     /in the ancient fogs & light/a hanging-on/

Think of it: a tree *3000 yrs. old*
          the long run of our WEST-SIDE STORY
where after gang fight the shadow 300ft. high in alley
& sprig to hold us wet/you/me/everyone/
          a moon planting

the rough bark of love in the sight of coyote where we run
                    /to catch each other's retrograde 19
     in the 12th house of ZODIAC/
                    a 3000 yr. *run* on LOVE

to the cliffs & geologic thunder in the *"dark place"* of the Pomos
     where we fireproof with adobe/   & from the sawpit
                    on a downstroke/pitman
                    & their women emerge in gold-rush-wild roses
under sea fog & valleys: *the palo colorado*
                    of their flesh

          in the CHURCH OF ONE Tree
     cut from a single redwood in Santa Rosa

Interest rates

       SO TO MY USA
with your tumbled buildings/your glistening WORDS
in mouth kissed on 34th in the NY spoof of our Parasite Cafe/
in your SPACES made for speed & cash: *go call up*
       your reserves/call out your troops
for the Wall St. Waterloo & significant plunge of futures/
film car-crash on a bridge & paint the Golden Gate green/
take back your pledges extracted from teeth on these roads!/
rip off the lid of L.A. & tunnel under Dixie to the sea—

The Sears Tower is bending to kiss the dead/& the red hawks
of Arizona have been found camped out in the Rotunda/
Lake Michigan whispers lottery in steel & the Pacific crawls to
       Santa Monica/without SHIVA

You have blessed your daughters with HEALTH in the foothold
of the grave/& your sons put on the hangman's hood/
The suits we buy are *flaming*/& our shoes are considerably plastic/
The walls are filled with wires & padded with rubber—so

       it's just first things first in the delivery of goods
before the daily HYPODERMIC of facts from asylums/
The rumble under our floorboards in offices of *execs* & the thunder
       of trucks/
Skulls bloom in the canyons & pine tree whispers in the elevator/

So carry your WEIGHT on the back of the Earth/Lift your own
       bales!
       —Take your Eyes off me & look to the mountains—

    My Gold USA . . . you have moved us to tears as we work,
       you have taken us by surprise in our beds/

and to the
exhausted mythologies/the neutrality of zero-degree violence
the slaughtered dreams in their quivering contralto

O STREETS OF MY ZOO!

where I walk to the dimmest of starlight in the sensuous disguise
of my triple-stitched jeans & shank buttons/
in the denim of gender & high value of Real as SPECTACLE:
to those HORIZONTAL for the mountains & monitored
by the scanners of retreat from our
dishes prepared by the *maitre de's* of technical kindness/

I give the ***mygrations***
I give the mygrations from the profile drag of the heart in careful
measurement of memory
driven in method to find its point strummed in the Ether—
a silent truth
in my estrangements & attachments